WHO BUILT THE BERLIN WALL?

History Book Grade 5

Children's Military Books

For 28 years, the Berlin Wall stood as a division between families, and as a symbol of the Cold War between Western democracies and Soviet Communism. Read about why it went up and how it came down!

THE NORMAN FOSTER REDESIGNED
GERMAN BUNDESTAG, BERLIN

WHY A WALL?

Germany has been a great power in Europe for centuries, but from the middle of the 1800s it worked hard to expand that power. Germany felt hemmed in by France and Great Britain to the west, which had large overseas empires, and the Soviet Union to its east.

Between 1870 and 1945 Germany fought three huge wars to try to expand its territory and influence.

It won the first, the Franco-Prussian War, in 1870, and gained territory from France. It lost World War I, which ran from 1914 to 1918.

ADOLF HITLER

The terms of the treaty ending World War I were harsh on Germany, and when the world economy entered the crisis called the Great Depression in 1929, forces in Germany called for the country to seize its rightful place of power again. Under Adolf Hitler, the National Socialist Party, or "Nazis", took power in Germany in the early 1930s.

By 1939, Germany had taken territory from France, Austria, and Czechoslovakia by threats of war. Finally, when Germany pretended that Poland had attacked it, and invaded Poland, other countries stood by Poland and World War II began.

GERMAN SOLDIERS INVADE POLAND, 1939

World War II ended with the defeat of Germany and its allies, including Italy and Japan, in 1945. The war had caused millions of deaths and untold suffering in many countries.

embers of the "Allies", the countries that defeated Germany, took control of Germany, dividing it in four parts.

The United Kingdom, France, the United States, and the Soviet Union each controlled a section of Germany. Its capital, Berlin, was divided the same way, even though Berlin was completely inside the sector controlled by the Soviet Union.

BOMBINGS OF HEILBRONN IN WORLD WAR II

COLD
WAR

A COLD WAR

The countries that had joined together to defeat Germany were not really all friends. The United States, France, and Great Britain were allied against the Soviet Union. The Soviet Union installed governments sympathetic to it in all the countries of eastern Europe, and what became known as East Germany. The two sides often threatened each other but their armies did not fight each other, so this period became known as the "cold war".

GERMAN RECOVERY

The three western sections of Germany became known as West Germany. The economy and people's lives began to recover there much faster than in East Germany. This was especially obvious in divided Berlin, where the eastern part of the city still looked shabby while the western part began to rebuild and recover its spirit.

BRITISH MILITARY HOSPITAL,
RINTELN, WEST GERMANY

MAINTAINING THE BERLIN AIRLIFT

The Soviet Union tried to starve the western armies out of West Berlin with a blockade of the city in 1948, but the Allies flew millions of tons of food and other supplies in to the city in the "Berlin Airlift". The Soviet Union gave up the blockade in 1949.

In 1958, the situation became worse again. Since 1949, more than three million East Germans had made their way to West Germany in search of a better life.

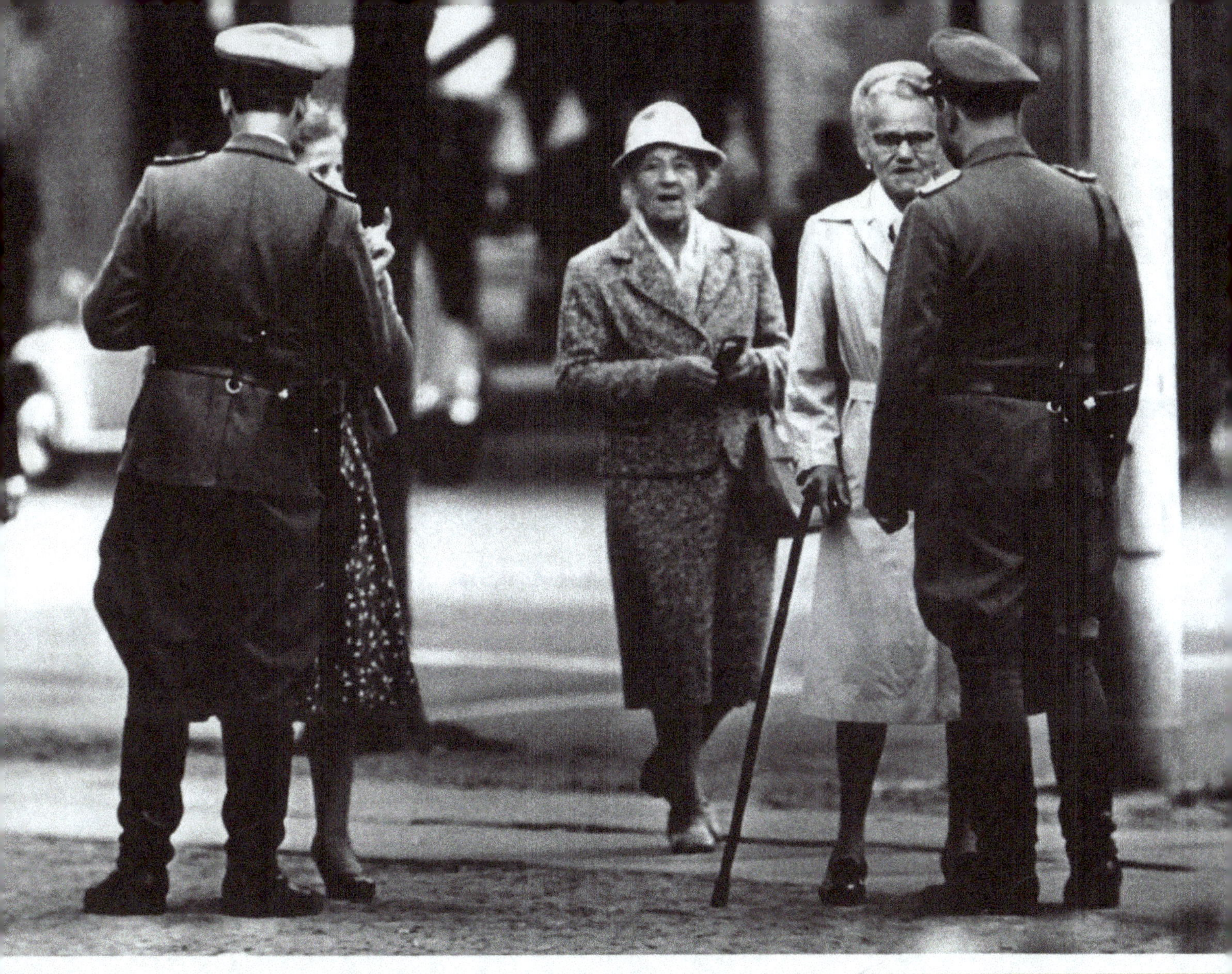

The rate of migration was growing quickly in 1961: on August 12 2,400 people crossed the border in a single day, the largest number ever.

WHEN THE WALL WENT UP

The night of August 12, 1961, Premier Khrushchev of the Soviet Union agreed to let the East German government close its borders. East German leader Ulbricht ordered the building of a wall of concrete and barbed wire to divide Berlin in half. Within two weeks the first Berlin Wall was in place.

ULBRICHT ORDERED THE
BUILDING OF BERLIN WALL

Up to that time, Berliners had been able to cross the border easily to go to work, to shop, or to visit family. Once the wall was up, normal people could not cross the border. People with special permission, such as government representatives, could pass through a checkpoint if they had the correct papers.

LIFE AND DEATH WITH THE WALL

Suddenly family members were cut off from each other, people could not continue their jobs or complete their college studies, and people could not get to shops and doctors they had been used to.

GERMANY IMMIGRATION CONFUSION

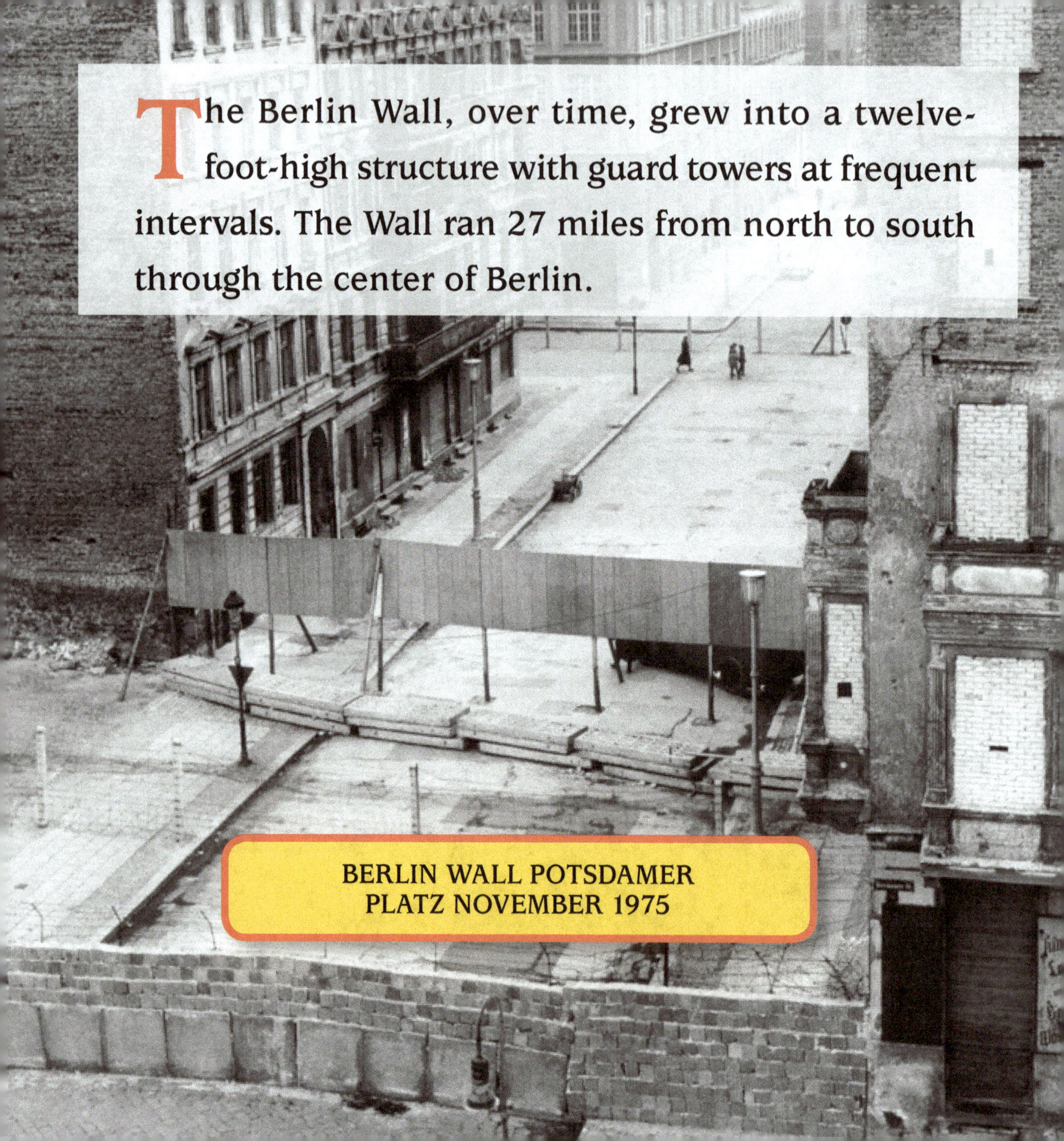

The Berlin Wall, over time, grew into a twelve-foot-high structure with guard towers at frequent intervals. The Wall ran 27 miles from north to south through the center of Berlin.

The ground on the east side of the Wall was cleared of buildings and other obstacles, and anybody approaching the Wall could be arrested or even shot.

Guards had orders to shoot on sight anybody trying to cross the border, and soldiers with attack dogs and machine guns patrolled up and down the Wall, supported by floodlights and more soldiers in the guard towers. People could only cross through checkpoints. The wall seriously slowed the flow of East Germans moving to the West, but it did not stop the flow altogether. Between 1961 and 1989 more than 5,000 East Germans made it across the border—including 600 border guards! People tunneled under the Wall or crawled through Berlin's sewer networks.

BORDER SECURITY IN STAAKEN

They tried to crash through weak points in the Wall with trucks, climbed over the barbed wire at the top of the Wall, or tried to float to the West using hot air balloons.

Three brothers named Bethke created a series of incredible escapes. Ingo Bethke floated across the Elbe River on an air mattress in 1975. In 1983, brother Holger used a bow and arrow to fire a steel cable to a roof top in West Berlin. Friends there made the cable secure, and Holger crossed high up above the Wall. Finally, in 1989, the first two brothers flew an ultra-light plane into East Germany to rescue their brother Egbert, and flew him safely to the West.

BERLIN WALL 1975

This was not all a merry adventure, though. Hundreds of people were imprisoned for trying to escape to the West, and almost 200 people were killed while trying to get through the Wall.

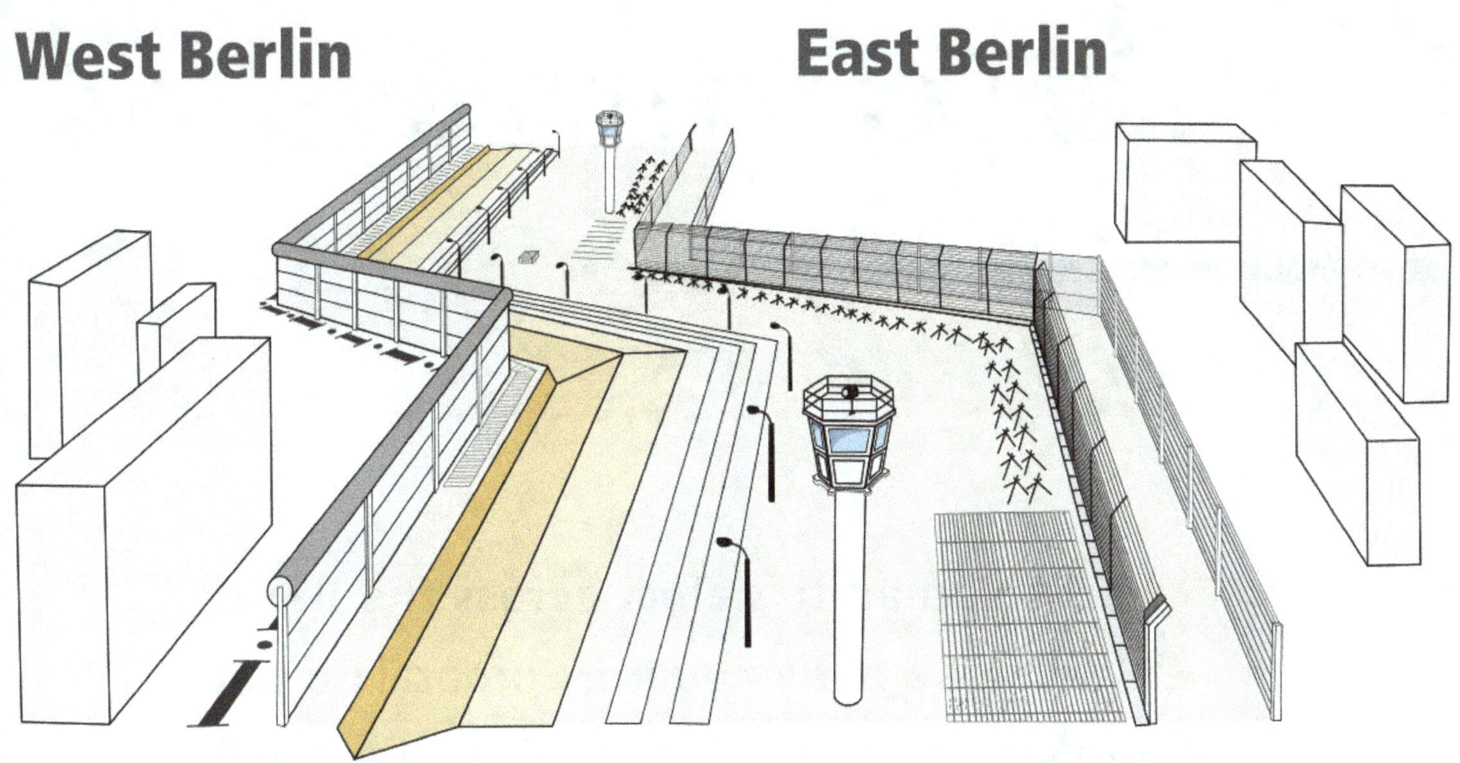

The Berlin Wall became a symbol of the hateful nature of the governing system of East Germany. Far from keeping them safe, the state was holding its people like prisoners.

BERLIN WALL FACTS

The first man to defect across the Berlin Wall was a border guard, Corporal Conrad Schumann. He jumped over a three-foot-high barbed-wire barrier two days after the Wall started to go up.

CORPORAL CONRAD SCHUMANN

BRANDENBURG GATE

The Berlin Wall included the Brandenburg Gate, which was built in 1791 to celebrate a triumph by Prussia, the eastern part of Germany. The Gate was in a wall that surrounded Berlin starting in the 1730s. The city has grown a lot since then!

The East German government claimed they had built the wall as a defense against attacks from the west. It claimed that spies and enemy agents had been sneaking into East Germany through Berlin to do terrible things, and that the Wall would stop them.

EAST GERMAN POLICE OFFICER

When the Berlin Wall first went up, many countries considered it a good thing. They did not like the Wall, or what the East German government was doing to its people, but at the time it seemed like the western countries were on the brink of war with the Soviet Union

and its allies. Many people, including United States President John F. Kennedy, felt that a terrible wall was far better than a war that would kill millions of people.

PIECES OF THE BERLIN WALL IN
THE POLLINATOR GARDEN

You can find pieces of the Berlin Wall in many places around the world. A part of the Wall still stands in a park in Berlin, as a memorial to those who died trying to cross it. As many as 40,000 sections of wall were recycled and used in new buildings. Several hundred pieces are in museums and private collections around the world—and one large piece is even in a bathroom in a casino in Las Vegas.

WHEN THE WALL CAME DOWN

By the late 1980s, the tensions of the Cold War were relaxing and countries of the Communist block started changing their relations with western countries. On November 9, 1989 the leadership of East Berlin said that, starting at midnight, East German citizens would be free to go through the checkpoints into West Berlin.

EINE WELT OHNE MILITAR ES GILT
TEILUNG DURCH BÜRGERRECHTE
LONG LIVE DALAI
THIS WALL

illions of people from both sides of the Wall gathered at it in celebration. At midnight, they flooded the checkpoint gates as they opened.

Nobody ordered the Wall to come down: people started attacking it with crowbars, hammers, and other home tools. Soon after, people started using bulldozers to knock down whole sections of the wall.

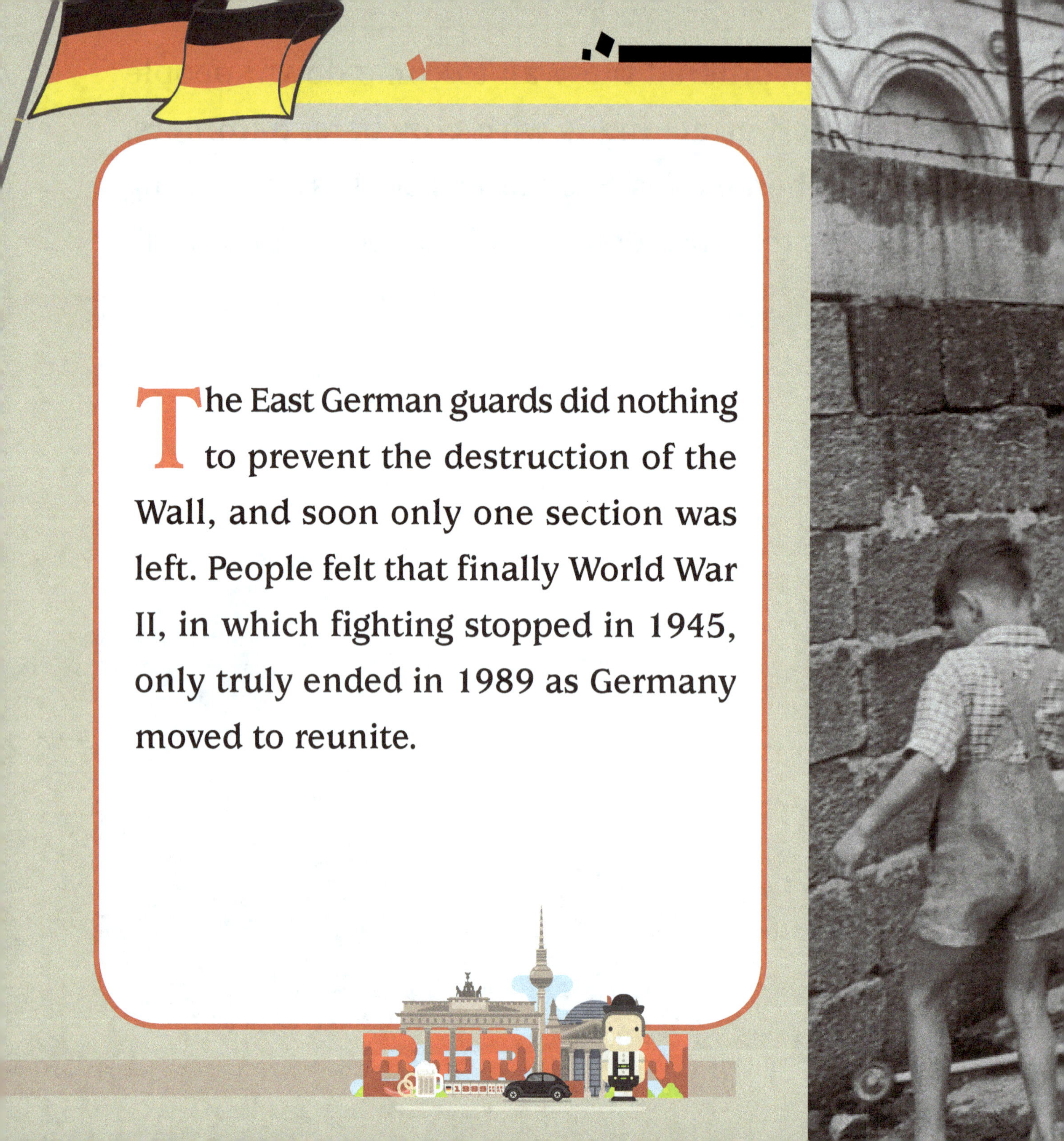

The East German guards did nothing to prevent the destruction of the Wall, and soon only one section was left. People felt that finally World War II, in which fighting stopped in 1945, only truly ended in 1989 as Germany moved to reunite.

WEST BERLIN WALL, 1962

RUINS OF BERLIN WALL IN TRURO

WALLS AND HUMAN SPIRIT

For almost 30 years the Berlin Wall stood to prevent people doing what they wanted to do, and as a symbol of the power of governments. When it came down, it became the symbol of what people can do when they refuse to accept oppression.

On November 9, 1989, people danced on top of the Wall and took it apart with any tools they could put their hands on. They turned a symbol of suffering into a symbol of hope and renewal.

ROMERO ARIAS
FREEDOM FOR
ACHTUNG!

I GOT
POL

Learn about another great wall, built for a different purpose, in the Baby Professor book Who Built the Great Wall of China?